Healing Hands of Women

Other Books by Steven Helmicki

The Ballerina with Brass Knuckles in Her Purse

Remedy Lane

Healing Hands of Women

Steven Helmicki

The World is spun by the momentum of women. This book is dedicated to DMH, CTH, BAG and JMP, all part of spinning me to a better place. My words cannot adequately express my gratitude. I am a better man from each of you. Any good I do is an extension of all of you.

A sincere debt of gratitude goes to my cover man Richard Walters Jr., whose creativity and insanity know no boundaries.

Behind everyman's smile is the supportive hand of a woman.

The Table of Contents

Ode

To someone

Rather the only one

Who sees healing

Under scabs

No picking

But nursing

Back to trusting

The World again

Seems to belong

To me.

Strange Love

Such a strange, exciting
Rub of the head
A comfort
An ease
An entanglement
A fragrance of curls
In a ball
A freedom
Decrease tension
Heart rates peak
Flutter
Relaxingly pumping comfort
Past extremities
Into the soul
The air is different
Breathing with you
Clear and measured
No last gasps
But the purity of oxygen
Your lavender
Whiffs me asleep
To a dream so peaceful
I don't want to awaken.

Pillow

So I hear the click
Of heels
Rapid steps
An urgency in a beautiful coat
A scarf
The tide of soothing smells
In front of me
Is beauty
Obvious and discreet
External and internal
All of it
So much of it
Luring everyone to envy
The place I lay my head.

Escaping

Got to have your attention
To closeness
Mine you hold
The value of disappearing
Inside you for moments
Escaping the pace of concern
The World has wrapped me
In its problems
But I dance with you
Hidden in the pockets of my jacket
Oblivious to the sirens
And chaos of my life.

Transferring

My feet practice the paces
Of deep disturbance
Unsettled drama
The tragedy of the stage less
Engrossed in accidents
Too little seen
A procrastinator's eye
A hand too late
A kiss blown goodbye
A goodbye blown
A comatose grandmother
Slipping away
The time in this life
My little girl's hand
Holding someone else
Will takeover
Leave off
To a place time served
People are better
By themselves
We all wait
To be taken
By love.

Tripping

Even a steady pace can be too slow
When life preys on your potential
Yesterday is clearer than today
Is one day past the due date
Opportunity expired but……..
There is this one thing
That's got me
Freedom in the night
My heart beat down embraced
To a sanctuary of acceptance
Some soft touch exploration
Healing the self-avoidance
That success tripped me up
Before I got there.

Hunger

So now I crave
Closeness that was unknown
Beyond words and other's experiences
Life suddenly justified and verified
Following the trail
Leading to secret places in your heart
Where I inhabit you
A place you can always feel
Finding me
Deep inside you
Whispering about your greatness
So you know
Always hold your head high
Never fear my hand is always
Reaching for you.

Enjoy Time

Circumstances are rivaled
Passion and parting
Time intertwined and escaping
We own not even our last breath
In the end is extended
To endure one last second
We give anything
But there is no trading back
Just the wisdom to enjoy now
The pleasures of freedom
The pleasures of passion
The richness of closeness
The will power to heal.

She Heals

A healing hand
On the temples
Tranquility appears
In front seats
A transformation of anxiety
Absorbed by the water
Edge of the night
A glimmer of peace
Black boots and stockings
An elegant scarf
Adolescent acts
The freedom of purity
No impulse
Just the desire of an elegant woman.

Tempting

So there can be
Intimacy in thought
Our minds close
But our wills unknown
What impulses may
Divulge about beliefs
Relative to various hungers
They are intertwined
Our addictions unknown
Until the hook
Sets us down denial
Tiring to the surface
Our aches will be known
Like a fish on its side
Vulnerable even to itself.

Bound Pages

The shelves hold

Undetermined knowledge

Of acceptance

Intelligence gathered

From back in time

One must go

To get to the future

Of our minds

Expands

Forward and backward

Abruptly polluted and restarted

Structured logically

To be driven by impulse

Grounded in great works

Only to question

That stripped down

Does any of it have legitimacy

In our time

Even we don't

Get to know

Until it is

All after but we get

Closest between the covers

The language of life
Leads us to our own truths
Even in other's footsteps
There is independence.

Chance

The beauty
Of passing traditions
That become some sort
Of uniqueness
A different life
We all succumb
To stretching for
The infinity of greatness
Improvement is only sub-conscious
There is always farther to go
But to know we are all going at all
Is knowing we are graced.

Self-forgiveness

A treaty with happiness
Must come
To anyone
Who will lead people
With sadness and hate
To anywhere great
Comes the path of relinquishing
The desire for suffering
Is not for toughness
But erosion of the soul
We must forgive ourselves
For being ourselves
Is not treachery
But a duty
To the difference
God creates all of us
Equally unique.

Unshakeable Journey

If it could be
So warm the rest
Of the way
Is still unclear
But hope in holiday jazz
Makes me future nostalgic
To ideals that maybe
Exist only in my head
But my mind's hope
Has uncharacteristically
Taken up residence
In the neighborhood
Of pessimism
Was an old way
To control destruction
Leave the attic lights
On all night
Making walking
To higher ground
Very possible.

Finding in Me

You pull me inside
Out of it comes pain and glory
Growth that rips away
From the past
I appear first crawling
Then limping
Then walking
Head down
Start to swagger
Soon looking everyone
Deep in their eyes
To see truth
Is the only way
A man can survive
The burning question
Of what does this life mean
In the background of time
Contemplating waste
Pacing extraordinary rhythms
Drive me outside relationships
Exploring intrinsically

From something that appears extrinsically
But it is so deep inside
It pumps one with my heart
Some days there is just
Coldness of the left chest
Walking on my own moon
The October of Life
Upon realization
This is not perpetual
Or even a long time
A Mother's words
Never let anyone
Bring you down
Reverberates everywhere
This late in the game
Is not for the past
But somehow the what ifs
Echo as if to ask myself
Why was I not listening.

Magic

I see

First grade glances

Notes exchanged

Grade school portraits

On blacktop holding hands

A shoebox of your brother's medals

Double on a banana bike

Back alley kisses

Tension begins so early

We compete

For the best girl

A phone number

A glance at an amusement park

Chasing the fastest

Behind portable classrooms

Exploration of anatomy

Desire begins

The life of long tension our drama.

Mom

I wish to give your childhood
Back if one thing
I had power
To reward what was stolen
From someone who was never
Selfish for me because I owe
You life
Mine the whole of it
The survival of it
My impression of the good of it
More than I can ever say
Thank you is trite
For a savior's support
Any greatness achieved
Truly a reflection
Of the good in you
The hope in you.

Why Couldn't I

Why couldn't I know you
Have my brother's face
And my shoulders
There was a time you
Smiled before death
Took you and the memories
Drank away
But a picture appeared
Looking at me from somewhere
Peacefully you choose
Not to interfere
But let me know
A proud grandpa rests.

Carson

You ignite
Sometimes my only happiness
Is that I had you
To watch become
A woman who changes
The world will be drawn
To you great responsibility
Will come following
Your own path
Down the unknown
To prove that goodness
Lays beyond anything
Earthly time will be
Outdone by my spirit
Inside of you
Papa guards
Your vulnerability
Pushing you
True to yourself.

Siesta

Rest is not
A lazy pastime
But a refocus
To climb
Real success
An embattlement
Tired soldiers
Succumb first
To themselves
Then to the world
Needs its leaders
Not battle wary
But full of the vigor
Necessary to achieve
The labeled impossible
Dreams of real visionaries
That somehow make
The world a better place
For even the I told you so's.

Strive

Used to love

The smell of erasers

Sharpened pencils

Fresh papers for ideas

They were valued

At least by me

Time brought none to fruition

But potential always

Leaves the door open

To success there are no quarters

Periods or time limits

Except death

All of us hopeful

It doesn't come too soon.

Living

I wanted pictures
To prove me worthy
Of the acclaim I sought
In the wrong way
Behind bars I never
Was one to believe
Anything less than being it
All is too much
A sentence
But one freely chosen
To take a bite of everything
Swallow life whole
It goes too fast anyway.

Maybe

In the night aloneness
Comfort comes to me
From your earlier presence
The perfume still there
Underneath my nose as if
You were still nearby
Maybe you listen for me
From far away
My footsteps soothe
You to stillness
I am warm to you
Like a distant light
You are drawn to me in darkness
Even though I am just a few shades
Lighter grey more from pain than from wisdom.

Love's Will

So they say free will
What of this love
Beyond my decision
It grabbed me
It consumed me
It drives me
To places of comfort
To an oasis of peace
No pretense
Just two souls entwined
In the flesh
Hearts slow down
To where they are hard
To tell apart.

Release

It is whistle blown dead
Intermission
A stop in the play of life
A little rewind and unwind
Just what the fuck happened
A collision of wills
The forfeiture of time
An alabaster face
Walking past beaded doorways
To the waterbed's tide flow
In smoky clouds
The mirror reflects
Grinding motions
In rhythm with bed waves.

I Can Sleep When I Die Fixing the World

So repeating to myself
The positive strangeness
Of the other side
Of pessimism I once declared citizenship
Now fleeing to peace
There's a happy side
To my path a strange warmth
Of little more than okay
But it steals hope
A flame where a flicker
One wind from being blown out
Flicked instantly
Toward a challenging
Self-proclaimed authority
The right thing resumed
In me the definition of success.

Reflections of Contentment

Apparently vicious
Once was I
Driven by vulgar emptiness
To brinks of death and destruction
A salvation of bullies
Was my mission to martyr happiness
Battling even those on my side
Contorted and tormented
Kicking and crawling
Into and out of arms
One flat after the next
A blonde, a brunette
My mother none of them
Lasted after the romance
Of whispers turned to hollers
Broke my heart to pieces
Too many times scattered
But even in broken glass
You can see windows to my goodness
Can soothe you despite my cuts
Even the deepest wounds heal

Maybe not all the way
But today I am driven
By happiness
Passing on the first red head
Wasn't passing at all
Have always been about
The insides are my misgivings
More than the next man
That I suffer so
With your questions
Must still find myself
A reflection of contentment.

Daughter

So a star was born
To me a little girl
In a yellow plastic sled
The big hill
Undaunted she always
Gets back on top
Can see she is more than four
An agent to beauty
Hysteria and will
Challenging to the status quo
Already seeking truth
The simplest common denominator of life.

Trade

So instances of snow
Trickles from the sunlight
Disappears like dust
From the tree branches
Night falls with a red tinge of warmth
The sky tricking us to comfort
Stillness resists cold winds
We must self-contain
The hard elements
Part of the trade
For any peace we get.

Determination

Some say it is gone
Covered unrecoverable
But everyone gets
At least two times
Trying the path will
Be a quiet loneliness
Like turning yourself off
Unplugging electric anger
An earthquake of charm
Draws the world closer
To fitting inside
Of myself
Everyone is surprised
To see less than a kilometer
Behind the very best
Have to wipe away tears.

The Old Days

So the question
Is played by the piano
A happy ending to a sad song
Singing along only makes tears
Harder to get close to you
Shivering for you and from you
I am delivered
Delayed your affections
For some strange pull
Away from me you come and go
Your love for me
Boiling your insides
Outside the poker face of resentment
Hope the piano man plays
The happy ending
The when you tap your foot
Crack a smile
About one of our great memories.

Knowing You

So the distance/ to your heart
Closes in/my eyes I see
An image of peace/still yet active
So alive yet silent/a transfer of nothing more
Than time is authentic/no obligations drive
The force of an unplanned/meeting of my heart
Is not so distant/from you I hear heart beats
From me I hear you/never with sadness
Forever with anticipation/one long dance
Never slowing/even when the music stops
My footsteps are in concert/with you a part
Whispering in your ear/keep going to the point
Of greatness/what I know of you.

Lady Support

An inspiration
Of healing
Only a woman can
Absorb the darkness
Until it's clear
That the pathway
Is one direction
Leading to her
A stop along greatness
The perfumed gift of comfort
All women have mother's hands
Everyman seeks their warmth
The necessity of emotional nourishment
That really is behind the success
Of all the good any one
Of us claiming to be strong
Is only a partial picture
Close inspection
Will find you
Holding us up
To the world.

The Old Way

Just once
All this inner peace
Beside myself
I am not used to
The un-turmoiled
Above ground they
Live on smiles and hope
While some choke and drown frowns
And despair
Panhandling for trouble
Always willing to make it a rainy day.

Past Love

Some hangers are empty

From long ago functions

Some gala

A fundraiser

For someone who never sees it

Together the same view

Left or right front or back

The opposite side of up

Down to last tries

A shot in the dark

One last roll

A Hail Mary

Into too many defenders

Of the other side

Picked off the last few beats

Emptying out hearts

Like closets with bare hangers

You can see things no longer there.

Fields of Contact

The offense
Is this some
Shifting strategy
A chess pawn
Lured towards
Undefined clarity
A musical in my
Head dances and weaves
To openings
Of desire
A tribesman to lust
Finally sitting still
At halftime
A spectator's view
Of the chronic
Shiftiness of life's
Pleasure calling
Back to new fields
New quarters
The play clock definitive
The game does not
Play on forever.

No Joe Average

Some oddly
Endangered story
Of rescue
And rehabilitation
It unfolds
Unlikely fashion
Height jokes and all
To be king of any hill
After falling so
Short ends are not
For me anymore
Time on pessimism
Is wasted on
All the volunteers
Who nursed me
To respectability.

Tributary

To ask
What's it
Like no
Indigestion of ideas
Protruding out
Everywhere and anywhere
Impulsive creativity
Designing stuck
A pattern of incompleteness
Has been repainted flesh
Of calm power.

The Landing

Almost crashing
Into rooftop
Escapes from fate
The engine somehow
Restarted pushing
Me higher
Sputtering
Closer to the
Ground no landing gear
Just drive
To be more than me
I fly a veteran
Of life's war
My cockpit
Speaks truth to me
Originality is propaganda
Stolen ideas
Are recycled genius
Identifying outside humanity
The lessons of life
Are taught by the most common of men
Even those of self-determined greatness
Are closer to the worker bee than could admit.

A Way

Skipper was
A singing dog
Howling my
Name was so
Full of different
Expectations
From people
No longer
With me
Childhood companion
A revelry to freedom
Shaking past
The propaganda of limitation
Only the good times
Take me to places
I would rather be
Successful being
A toast to childhood pets
To the quiet after violence
That is filled with
The hope
It is all over
Living for someone else.

On a Prayer

Entranced on a line

Of cars passes

Down Main

Glances flash

Transparent through

Subway doors

Lead to nowhere

The excuse of getting

Away with another opportunity

Not to be blown

Changing lines

Into the direction

Of flirtation

I ride fantasy

Closer to reality

The impulse

Is love.

Dollar and a Dream Song

So through the glass
Staring at the covers
List of songs
A credit past seven
Looking for meaning
In the heart of this machine
Takes me back through time
Playing back life
In a corner bar
All the tears
Aren't for sadness
But those happy times
That make us smile
As we drive past
Pull up
To the end of time
Listen closely
This is your song.

Oxygen

Breathe

Back into me

You do

Turning

Your lips bite mine

And passionately

Erase doubt

Your hands

Ease hard

Times for softness

Sleeping here

Is home

For a moment

The world

Stops shaking

The life out of me

 Is you.

Baptism

A spiritual ness
In the smell of her
Hair I lose myself
To comfort
The guard down
Hair around
My face I slide my
Hands to her legs
Are like a shore
After a too long swim
Holding on
Been away from love
Breathless
My own poison
Is washed from
Within the euphoria
A light shines
Through my eyes
Of blackness
To the depths
You follow it to
Bright colors
Under fathoms of defenses

Exists the loving me
Vulnerable to rescue
Eagerly swimming
To the surface
Unknown whether to laugh or cry
Happiness is an adventure
To isolated goodness.

Road Less Traveled

A paved road
Is awaiting
From the overgrown
Path of treachery
Turn on and lead
To humanness
You will find
Even pessimists
Are treated well
In some neighborhood
We may even get happy
About the little things
Like the smell of food
And the sound of traffic.

Victory Drive

Over passed looking
Up there isn't
The answer
From the hectic
Driver I may
Look stranded
But the freedom
To maneuver
Is one a consumer
Never has
The right empathy
 Is for themselves
A foot in the trap
A lifetime
Of a race
Of victory once
Unknown.

Birthday Desire

I want to approach you anonymously
From the rear
But my footsteps give me away
To your memory submitting
You bend to my want
Over solid objects you brace
I take from you fear
And pump freedom
Into your warm core
You quiver
And throb
You are more than tasting
You are devouring the will
Of desire.

Sexual Healing

Anticipation of urgency
Relieved on her back
Lays comfortably
Accepting thrusts
Of frustration
Over time
Pumping freely
Of lustful volition
Riding far away
From past realities
Let resentment go
Flows from everything
Up to that point
In time
Needs again
The company
Of a beautiful woman.

Don't Stop the Time/Live it

I threw away time
To make it go faster
To the end of the road
There is no magical peace
To be found outside ourselves
We must climb
To see the other side
Is full of grief too
Just less expected
And more painful
Our personal hells
Were mere purgatory
To the truly disenfranchised
Who sell their children to eat
What we turn our noses at
That somehow our bad
Is worse than third world poverty
Waste no more opportunity
For freedom exists
In only small pockets of the world
Do we have this chance.

Hope

So the noise

Of water usually

Relaxes me

But my fish tank's echo

Underscores

Dead silence

Ghosts of our past

Dance in the form

Of memories

Are but we

Anymore

Anxious I am

For you

Tell me one

Way or the other

We have history

To preserve

It must be

Just salvation

Can come even

In the small air

Of a whisper

A millisecond of a glance

Start there and work
Toward forward
Progress is
Both of us happy.

Last Piece

So you are this puzzle piece
That fits perfectly in the light and darkness
Complimentary and so real like my shadow
One that I can taste and smell
To completeness you are necessary
Hanging on me
Attached to me
I move forward
Braver
Bolder
Happier.

A New

Dream beyond anything
You can see
Ahead of yourself
Is not the distance
Of time travel
But a small reach
To success taking
Hold of destiny
Is what separates
Victory from potential
The consistent climb
Outside our skin
To new realities.

Love's Protection

The intensity stops
Oblivious to surrounding
Stares and danger
The energy
A protective wall of sanity
In the bustle of the world
We are an island
Impenetrable to hate
Jealousy makes us smile
The way to a cure
Is the display
Of dance steps
Not letting the world
Eat more of you than necessary.

It's Both

Dedications are pleas
For acceptance to the core
We expose not for fame
But to offer what little
A poet can to the world
But the wisdom
Of happiness and pain
They are kin
In this existence
Smiles and tears intersect
But that doesn't make it
Any less spectacular
To be alive.

Championed Self

A fantastic finish
Is the sweeping
Turnaround of the underdog
Made to believe
A place in the class
Of unsuccessful was a permanent
Graduation to failure
Is a psychological state
Meant to be temporary
The final run through
Is to glory
Of escaping opinion
To the undeniable podium
Of our own completeness.

Model

On a cat
Walk to
And from
Me you desire
The passion
In your steps
Closer to me
Extending beauty
Beyond flashes
And applause
Ranting in the rags
Clean up costs
Even the glamorous
Love danger
Attributed to themselves
The notion
Of impurity.

Two Women

So the hard side
Of indifference
Is going through
The motions
But claiming
You are really there
Elsewhere in laughter
You chuckle at greatness
I am a crooked tree
To my leaves
Are falling
My roots rotten
You indifferently suck
Until my core
Is empty of both good and bad.

You heal me
By twisting me
In every position
You clean my core
Emptying hostility
Into it is recycled
To hope and well being

Fixing what's broken
Is just a methodical
Course of relaxing pleasure
I watch flesh
Traveling vertically
In the dark
Leather supports
Both determination
And desire
To let go of everything
And start over loving ourselves.

The Female Drive

A constant drive
On what fuel
Is this need
To perfect life
A woman's view
Of the preciousness
Birth creating the scenario
For hope that understanding
Comes from the cradle
Spinning the music of success
Mothers planning escape
From the traps that
Hold them in place
Run child run
Towards the light
There are warmer places
Than this town
Than this house.

The Smell of Each Other

The story of love

Is not so tragic

In reality

We find

A difference

From the fairytale

Tells us anything

Flawed is obsolete

We dispose of our dreams

Wrongly seeking perfection

When the magic we seek

Breathes in our bad habits

Mutually willing to

Accept a little less

The truth.

Stick People

The Art of our mystery

Is in its simplicity

No pretensions

The aspersions of others

Silently pass us

Our music too captivating

To consider the downside

We dance until the music stops

Only when we decide

Will what others say

Matter to reality never

Discount the truth

About finding love

In the most unlikely places

Seeking you is pleasure

For my soul.

Kodak Moment

Find a picture
Of me smiling
It's my real place
Un-conflicted
It wasn't me
Responsible for
All tragedy
Could hardly fix
My own lies
Are forgiven
Trust me I've
Paid with some potential
Time dedicated to myself
Was impossible
Too long
Diminished by my shadow
Projecting hope.

Evelyn Gauloise Paris 1958

Exhale a toxic puff
Your lips desire
Your eyes shift
A face void of truth
Easy to see
How any one
Would lift the veil
Resuscitating your smile
Sucking the mystery
Out of you
Too beautiful
For pain
Of love
I will stand
Taller than me
In spaces you
Will find peace
Back in a picture
Moment I am drawn
Into your mouth
Smoke of me
Fills your lungs
A Jeanie

Three wishes
I grant you me
Even today.

The Sun Also Rises

Like sun damage
Old love
Broken exposure
Accumulating in me
I hide shaded
By denied emotion
But the draw of warmth
Always strips me naked
Free to the core
Trying again
At purpose
You can glow
And smell of the sea
I will drown in you
Bake from you
Each new day
Drawn to me
Silence in my ear
The first peace
In my life
With a woman
Somewhere brighter
Than the solitude of dark.

Where Men Really Go

In front are books
Claiming wisdom
To me raised by
A quotable woman
Mothers occupy libraries
The answers to love
Are learned and forgotten
Early in a matronly lap
Kindness sometimes
Only comes at gravesites
To you say
Wake up
To those tender words
Even if they are from memory
They are your path.

www.ingramcontent.com/pod-product-compliance
Lightning Source LLC
LaVergne TN
LVHW011411080426
833311LV000003B/488